Greenway

Devon

THE NATIONAL TRUST

DEVON'S SECRET GARDEN

SITED ON a promontory above the River Dart, Greenway is an evocative landscape with a rich history and mystical atmosphere.

The jewel of the estate is the glorious woodland garden which time seems to have passed by. Gardened for 400 years by quirky, passionate plantsmen and women, Greenway has evolved into a charming secret garden held on the edge of wildness and harbouring a nationally significant plant collection. It was given to the National Trust in 2000 by Rosalind and Anthony Hicks and Mathew Prichard.

The characters involved in Greenway have often been as important and as eccentric as the garden they created. They include explorers, merchants, a soldier, MPs, a copper magnate and a world-famous crimewriter, Agatha Christie,

and her archaeologist husband. It was her daughter and son-in-law, Rosalind and Anthony Hicks, who have most significantly contributed to the garden as we see it today.

Successive owners enjoyed Greenway as a second home, all adding to the layers of its history, but each approaching it with a sense of relaxed responsibilities. They have made it an enchanted, mysterious garden, in which the mild Devon climate, and the peaceful rhythm of season and river ebbing and flowing, have helped to create a sense of wildness and timelessness. The result is an atmosphere of calm solitude, which the Hickses have striven to preserve.

Above Magnolia kobus

Left View of the Dart Estuary from the garden

Right Greenway House *c.*1910, when it was much more exposed

THE GILBERTS: 15th century–c.1700

First mentioned in 1493, 'Greynway' was the crossing point of the Dart to Dittisham. In the late 16th century, a Tudor mansion, Greenway Court, was built for Otho Gilbert and his wife Katherine, née Champerknowne. Tristram Risdon, a local historian, described it as a 'delightful dwelling', having extensive views of the estuary below. Of their three children born at Greenway, Sir Humphrey, a favourite of Elizabeth I, took possession of Newfoundland for the Queen, whilst Sir John became a lord lieutenant of the county and a man of great local influence, remaining at Greenway for his lifetime.

THE ROOPES: c.1700–91

Roope Harris Roope probably built Greenway House, the central block of today's building, next to Greenway Court. Recent excavations near the house exposed the foundations of what must have been the Court. A merchant adventurer, Roope developed trade with the New World, possibly importing plants and seeds from America and Portugal – a relation of his having introduced the *Camellia* 'Captain Rawes'.

THE ELTONS: 1791–1832

Edward Elton, Bristol merchant adventurer and MP, paid over £9,000 for the property, which, according to a 1791 plan, comprised the new house, two enclosed gardens, a fountain garden and drying yard, behind which the Court had stood.

James Marwood Elton succeeded his father in 1811. He added two wings to the house and landscaped the surrounding garden. The original entrance to the property from Maypool was incorporated into the garden, and a realigned stretch of road was routed down the hill to a new entrance drive and lodge. This landscape in the style of the designer Humphry Repton remains much the same today.

Also dating from this era are some of the garden buildings, the beech trees, enclosing belts and the Camellia Garden. By the time the estate was sold in 1832, it included an extensive kitchen garden of one acre, a melon ground, flower gardens and, surrounding them all, 'a park of much natural beauty', the whole offering 'the appearance of enchantment rather than reality'.

COLONEL EDWARD CARLYON: 1832–51

Carlyon bought the estate for £18,000, but his tenure was shortened by the need to return to his Tregrehan estate, and he sold at auction for only £15,500. An account book written in the 1840s had noted substantial payments to nurseries, including Veitch, Lucombe and Prince, for plants possibly destined for Greenway, which could have included camellias and Turkey oaks for the newly created Camellia Garden, and the magnificent *Liriodendron* (tulip tree) near the house.

Above 1839 cartouche of Greenway

Greenway overlooking the River Dart by William Payne, c.1788

Right 1791 Estate map of Greenway

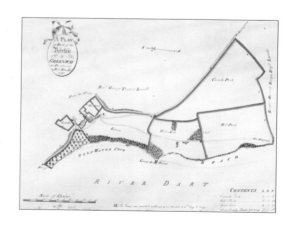

SIR
HVMFRY
KNIGHT·
IN·THE·
OF·VIR
ANN

NON

Left Portrait of Sir Humphrey Gilbert at Compton Castle, *c.*1584. He took possession of Newfoundland for the Queen, and was half brother of Sir Walter Ralegh.

Three further generations of Gilberts lived at Greenway, until a later Humphrey withdrew to his family seat at Compton Castle (now also owned by the National Trust), selling Greenway to Thomas Martyn. From Martyn the property passed to Roope Harris Roope, whose family originated from Dittisham.

Above *Trachycarpus fortunei*
and *Rhododendron arboreum*

Mr Joseph Henry Murley,
Head Gardener at Greenway
for the Bolithos and
Williamses with his son
William and friend, *c.*1914

Right Mr J. H. Murley, with
his family outside South
Lodge, *c.*1900–10

RICHARD AND SUSANNAH HARVEY: 1851–82

A wealthy copper magnate from St Day in Cornwall, Harvey set about modernising and expanding the estate, restoring the lodge and stables and adding two glasshouses to the walled garden, perhaps inspired by his cousin, Michael Williams, who was restoring Caerhays Castle. His gardener, J. Couldrey, wrote to *Gardeners' Chronicle* noting the fine specimens of exotic plants at Greenway, which included Acacia, *Clianthus*, *Sophora* and myrtles.

Harvey had fought a proposal for a railway to run across Greenway land down to Greenway Quay from where passengers could travel on to Dartmouth by boat. A compromise was agreed with the building of the Greenway tunnel that runs under Greenway and today transports tourists along the steam railway from Paignton to Kingswear.

THE BOLITHOS AND WILLIAMSES: 1882–1937

Thomas Bolitho of Trewidden bought Greenway for £44,000. A keen plantsman, he introduced the Cornish influence in the garden, specialising in camellias, magnolias and rhododendrons sheltered by laurel plantings.

Articles by S. Wyndham Fitzherbert in the *Gardeners' Chronicle* and *The Garden* (1899 and 1901) record numerous other varieties and species. Notable trees included *Cryptomerias*, Monterey pines, acacias and eucalyptus. More tender plants are *Gevuina avellana*, *Embothrium coccineum*, callistemon and phormium, and flowering climbers such as *Abutilons*, and Banksian and China roses.

After Bolitho's death in 1919, his daughter, Mary, and her husband, Charles Williams of Caerhays, took over Greenway. Charles was a prolific gardener and they planted extensively, especially rhododendrons, daffodils and magnolias from the nurseries at Caerhays and Werrington near Launceston, including several introductions discovered by the plant hunter George Forrest. Notes from Charles's planting notebook for 1916 to 1935 show that he was also ordering from the Veitch nurseries.

In 1937 the Williamses returned to Cornwall, leaving a more colourful and varied Greenway, which they sold to Sir Alfred Goodson of nearby Waddeton Court. The estate was split up, and within only a year the house with 36 acres was up for sale again for £6,000.

The Fountain Garden was added by the Harveys

View downstream of the River Dart from Greenway, *c.*1900

MRS MALLOWAN: 1938–59

Agatha Christie (known locally by her married name, Mrs Mallowan) could not resist buying Greenway. She and her husband Max, who was later knighted for his services to archaeology, soon became very attached to the place. It became their holiday home. Both were keen gardeners, ordering from Veitch, Treseder and Hillier. Even after the outbreak of war, Max continued listing wild flowers in the garden. In April 1942, his garden book noted the exceptionally late season, with camellias, magnolias and even primroses only just coming out.

During the autumn of 1943, Greenway was requisitioned by the Admiralty for the use of the United States Navy. As part of the preparations for D-Day, Greenway became the Officers Mess for the 10th US Patrol Boat Flotilla based in the Dart Estuary. Amongst them was a Lt Marshall Lee, who was to become their unofficial war artist, creating a frieze around the walls of the library. During the build-up to D-Day, American music could often be heard wafting over the estate. According to local rumour, an abrupt silence foretold another raid by the Luftwaffe!

ROSALIND AND ANTHONY HICKS AND MATHEW PRICHARD: 1959–2000

In 1959 the property was transferred by Mrs Mallowan to her daughter Rosalind Hicks, and from then until 2000 it was owned in various partnerships by her, her second husband, Anthony, and her son, Mathew Prichard. During this period the family purchased Lower Greenway Farm, comprising 109 hectares (270 acres), which completely surrounds the garden.

Anthony Hicks ran a commercial nursery at Greenway propagating plants grown in the garden. This in turn led to the creation of an increasingly specialised collection of tender and rare southern hemisphere plants in a natural setting. Rosalind and Anthony have lived at Greenway since 1967 and have greatly enjoyed the garden and their involvement in developing its unique characteristics.

In 2000, the family decided to give this much-loved family home and garden, including Lower Greenway Farm, to the National Trust.

Above View from the Tennis Court garden

Right In 1943, a Lt Marshall Lee from the United States Navy painted a frieze in the Library at Greenway. Greenway house is visible through the trees on the right

FALMOUTH ~ DARTMOUTH ~ ENGLAND

'We went over to Greenway, and very beautiful the house and grounds were. A white Georgian house of about 1780 or 90, with woods sweeping down to the Dart below, and a lot of fine shrubs and trees– the ideal house, a dream house…'

Agatha Christie

Above and left Agatha Christie and her husband, Max Mallowan, the archaeologist, at Greenway, 1946

9

Above *Magnolia campbellii*.
Greenway is famous for
its magnolias

Trachycarpus fortunei

Right Doorway leading from
the Putting Green into the
Plantation

FOLLOWING the generous gift of Greenway, the acquisition was secured with funds raised by the Neptune Coastline Campaign. The 121-hectare (300-acre) estate comprises Greenway House and garden, Lower Greenway Farm and adjoining parkland and woodland, much of which fronts the River Dart.

The Trust aims to keep the spirit of the place, its almost wayward character, its atmospheric beauty, and its timelessness and 'lost' qualities. Time will be taken to develop and nurture the garden to retain the excitement, the mystery and the wildness. Greenway will not be a 'found lost garden'.

To help piece together the jigsaw of Greenway, we have been able to use magnificent resources: the donor family, who have known the estate for 60 years; two previous head gardeners and one gardener, who have between them notched up 88 years work on the gardens at Greenway.

All have contributed to and supplemented the surveys commissioned by the Trust.

Surveys have been carried out by Trust specialists and external contractors on Greenway's garden history, archaeology and horticulture. The garden has been measured and mapped with the tagging of 2,700 significant trees and woody plants. Already much has been done, but there is much still to do. We have a ten-year plan of restoration, renovation and innovation.

We aim to conserve Greenway's plants and history, repair and restore paths and buildings, and enable others to discover this magical garden and the wider estate.

In 2002 the National Trust launched the Greenway Appeal for £1.1 million in order to save buildings such as this now derelict vinery. Every donation, whatever its size, will help us to protect this unique place. As visitors to the property enjoy the past, present and future labours, we hope they will contribute to the appeal and help us to help Greenway.

Left View of the Dart Estuary downstream

THE DART ESTUARY

THE DART ESTUARY consists of a tidal river cutting deep into the tranquil south Devon countryside.

The regular steamer service that once plied the river between Dartmouth and Totnes has now given way to the present-day river boats providing an important service – green transport into a green environment. Greenway's visitors today have the choice of arriving by boat.

Right **Greenway Quay**

Since Saxon times, the estuary has provided the necessities of life for generations of farmers, fishermen, merchant traders and mariners. Protected by the high hills at its mouth, the Dart's deep natural harbour has given mariners a safe haven and anchorage for centuries. The Normans developed it into one of England's most important trading ports. However, the river took merchant ships a further ten miles into the hinterland of south Devon – a tidal highway for the trade in tin, cloth and slate, centred around the inland port of Totnes. The influence of the estuary and its

trading towns became so important that in 1338 Edward III safeguarded its royal association by presenting 'the waters of the Dart' to his son, the Black Prince. The Dukes of Cornwall have inherited the title ever since.

Over the centuries, the estuary provided other resources for man's benefit, from the sands of its bed, to salmon making their way upstream to spawn in their ancestral Dartmoor waters. Today, the greatest resource that we have inherited is that of the Dart's timeless natural beauty.

Left Detail from a bird's eye view painting of the Dart Estuary by George Spencer Hoffman at Coleton Fishacre. Greenway is on the right at the top .

The Dart Estuary has become one of Britain's most popular tourist attractions. Over 100 years ago Queen Victoria was one of the first tourists to sail upstream and described the river as an English Rhine. These days the Dart has its own vineyard to complement that statement.

13

TOUR OF THE GARDEN

The Main Drive

At the entrance to Greenway is the Lodge, a single-storey, pale stone building in the Italianate style with a vaulted stone porch. The 1850 date stone carries the crest of the Harvey family, the Cornish chough.

The drive was laid out during the Elton period. It is considered to be Reptonian and remains largely intact. Planting is from the late 19th century onwards and includes a huge clump of *Eucryphia cordifolia* and *E.* x *hillieri* 'Winton'; *Rhododendron augustinii*; and a magnificent *Michelia doltsopa*, glorious in late spring with its scented white flowers. Almost opposite are *Quercus dentata* (a Williams planting) and *Q. mongolica*, which have remarkably large leaves. A *Quercus* x *hispanica* 'Lucombeana' is further down behind the walled garden. In places the shrubs open out into grassy glades, with glimpsed views to the park. The main drive follows the River Dart around the edge of the property and offers lovely glimpses of the river and Dittisham through the trees. A beautiful *Sequoia sempervirens* – the Californian Redwood – marks the end of this walk.

The Visitor Reception building

Opposite the Redwood is a bed of azaleas and magnolias on the corner of the stable block, which is now the Visitor Reception. This building dates in parts from the 18th century and was later remodelled by Harvey, who added the bell-tower and clock, dated 1852, and the colonnaded veranda. Stalls and loose boxes survive inside, though the carriage houses (now the lavatories and shop) were used as garages from around 1920, when the last horses left the property. Behind this building is the Barn (now the Café and Gallery), in which a petrol-run generator provided electricity for the estate until the 1950s. A pair of *Crinodendron hookerianum* stand in the yard; placed some years ago in limbo, they took root through their pots, which can still be seen today.

A *Drimys winteri* var. *chilensis*, at the corner of the stable block, is a handsome evergreen, which has fragrant, ivory white flowers in May. A tall shrub, which is actually a small tree, it is underplanted with *Eucryphia cordifolia* x *lucida* and *Fuschia* 'Mrs Popple'.

Above Rising above azaleas and magnolias are the clock and bell-tower on top of the stables and visitor reception

Right Michelia doltsopa on the main drive

Left Daffodils and magnolia tree on the banks of the entrance drive

Above Child evacuees playing by the tennis court. Greenway was let as a home for evacuees in 1942

Below The old peach house

The Tennis Court

En route to the Tennis Court is the *Magnolia campbellii*, planted by Max Mallowan in 1938. He waited some 20 years for it to bloom, often writing home to enquire about its progress. It has spectacular pink flowers in early spring.

At the entrance to the Tennis Court is *Itea ilicifolia*, an evergreen, holly-like shrub. In late summer it is laden with long drooping catkin-like racemes (hanging flowers), which are fragrant and greenish white. In the garden a *Davidia involucrata* var. *vilmoriniana* or Handkerchief tree is conspicuous in May; next to it is *Cercis siliquastrum*, the Judas tree. The tennis court is a 'Tennis Quick' court, one of the first all-weather courts of its type.

Cross the road to enter the South Walled Garden.

The South Walled Garden

Originally a kitchen garden and latterly a commercial nursery, the borders around the lawn contain some rare and beautiful species. Against the wall behind the herb border is an ancient *Wisteria sinensis*, a sea of pale blue in the spring. Beyond the Vinery, *Acacia verticillata*, with its yellow blooms, and the outrageously thorny *Colletia paradoxa* vie with other exotics. In the lawn in front of the Vinery is *Sophora tetraptera* 'Little Baby', and at the end of the garden in the raised border there are acacia, *Iochroma* and *Leptospermum*. Opposite the Vinery the border contains fine specimens of *Azara microphylla* and *Quillaja saponaria*, amongst others.

The Vinery was built in the early 19th century, and the *Gardeners' Chronicle* of 1901 noted that it was used for growing grapes until it became a 'stove house' for very exotic plants. It is a glasshouse with curved ends, abutting a traditional potting shed. These buildings and the South Walled Garden are the subject of a major restoration programme.

Walk through the top right-hand arch to the North Walled Garden.

The North Walled Garden

This continues as a working nursery garden, where plants are propagated for Greenway, with any surplus being offered for sale to visitors. Particularly notable is the group of figs, planted by Bolitho as standards. The Peach House, built in the mid-19th century, is the longest in Devon. Delicious peaches and nectarines were grown until 2000 and it is planned to continue this tradition once restoration is complete.

Follow the path to the right up to the Putting Green.

Above *Abutilon* 'Ashford Red'

Left The Vinery

The Putting Green

This garden takes its name from the Clock Golf course, laid out here in the 1940s, on which the family played in the long summer evenings. There is a border of hellebores in the spring and one of dahlias in the summer, planted by Agatha Christie and not lifted since. The shrub borders contain a fine *Buddleja colvilei* and the rare *Vallea stipularis*, which has small, deep pink flowers in early summer. Shading the lawn on the edge of the Fernery are a mature *Cornus kousa* and the choice white form of *Cercis siliquastrum*.

The Fernery

The Fernery or Fountain Garden was remodelled in the mid-19th century by Susannah Harvey. This enclosed garden of water-worn limestone and quartz, and spidery paths and central pool with fountain, is planted with ferns and has a cool, subdued atmosphere. A more melancholic ambience is created with the graves of more recent, much-loved dogs along the western boundary.

The Hydrangea Walk

A path leading away from the Fernery, between box hedges, is planted with tender rhododendrons for spring scent, and hydrangeas for late summer colour. Whilst the path leads on to the Top Garden, a turning to the right leads under a large Monkey Puzzle tree to the *Mother and Child* statue.

The *Mother and Child* Statue

This sculpture is by Bridget McCrumm, and was kindly given to the National Trust by Rosalind Hicks. It reclines on a field of *Cyclamen repandum* and narcissi.

Retrace your steps to the top path leading up to the Top Garden.

The Top Garden

The path leads through what was parkland in the Elton era. More recently planted with specimen trees, there are *Davidia, Ailanthus, Quercus* and, notably the Paulownias (Foxglove tree), which have purple flowers in late spring. There are one or two shrubberies, containing Corylopsis, camellias and Osmanthus.

The Top Garden was the last part of the park to be subsumed by the garden during the mid- to late 19th century. It commands a spectacular view of the Dart Estuary towards Dartmouth and Kingswear. The top border is a real sun-trap and is a riot of Crinums, Agapanthus, Anenomes and the Californian Poppy, *Romneya coulteri*.

A route for those who do not wish to tackle the steep hill down (and later up) is to follow the plantation back to the Visitor Reception. Exit the Top Garden through the gap in the wall and cross the concrete path to the Plantation.

Above Bridget McCrumm's statue of *Mother and Child*

The Hydrangea Walk

Left Joseph Murley, Head Gardener, in the Rose Walk, Greenway, c.1890. This feature no longer exists, but it was probably where the Hydrangea Walk is today

The Plantation

The grass path winds down round what used to be very heavily forested woodland. There are some younger plantings of Azara, Podocarpus and magnolias mixed in with some older Williams plantings of rhododendrons and crinodendrons.

Either return to Visitor Reception via the gate through to the Putting Green and Walled Gardens or walk up the concrete path to return to the Top Garden.

The Far End Path

From the Top Garden walk downhill along the path next to the eastern boundary of the shelter belt. As you descend, you pass under two venerable *Griselinia littoralis* amongst magnolias and Drimys. The views of the river from the terraces further down are glorious.

Carrying on downhill *en route* for the Bird Pond, you reach a clump of *Phyllostachys nigra* (Black Bamboo) at the top of a short path, a diversion to a stone well head, which is dated 1840. Returning to the main path again, you pass a *Dicksonia antarctica*, the evergreen tree fern nestling by a *Magnolia delavayi*, which was planted by Bolitho around 1880. It fell over in a storm some years ago and was cut back; what you see now is regrowth of only ten years. In front of this are *Gunnera manicata* and the pond.

The Bird Pond

The sculpture *Greenway Bird* by Bridget McCrumm, was given to the National Trust by Rosalind Hicks. The air here on a hot summer's day is thick with insect sounds – suitable companions to the bird.

From the Bird Pond either walk back towards the tree ferns, turning left down a narrow path past a double trough, and follow the Camellia Walk to the lower, Kwan Yin, pond. Or walk across the front of the pond and on to the middle path.

The Bluebell Bank

As you walk towards the house, the garden once again opens into parkland with steep banks of primroses and bluebells in spring. There are good specimens of *Parrotia persica*, *Cornus controversa* and *Rehderodendron macrocarpum*. The magnificent *Liriodendron tulipiferum*, the Tulip tree, with yellow- and green-banded flowers in June, is close to two large *Cryptomeria* cultivars, which form glades of layered branches.

The zig-zag path takes you back to the Top Path to return to the Visitor Reception. Walk back along the middle path to the Primrose Bank, avoiding the first path to the right. Follow the gentle descent amongst Cornus, myrtle and camellia, which form an understorey to some fine Northofagus.

The Kwan Yin Pond

The sculpture by Nicholas Dimbleby, given to the National Trust by Rosalind and Anthony Hicks, casts a discreet gaze through camellias, buddlejas and rhododendrons to the river beyond.

Walk downhill past *Podocarpus salignus*, a lush pile of willow-like foliage, *Azara serrata* and Eucryphia, all South American in origin, and bear left amongst beech and Sweet Chestnut down to the river, past a sunken feature and on to the River Walk. There is a fine view down to Noss, and then the path turns right to the Boathouse and on to the Battery.

Greenway's boathouse is a historical enigma bracketed between Tudor myth and legend and 20th-century fiction; and yet it is also a functional building.

Top right The interior of the Boathouse

Right The Battery

Ralegh's Boathouse

The boathouse is often referred to locally as 'Ralegh's Boathouse'. Sir Walter Ralegh, apparently, one morning was smoking a pipe at Greenway, when a servant threw ale over him, thinking he was on fire. As half-brother to Sir John Gilbert, Ralegh was closely involved in affairs of exploration and trade, and it is possible that a structure stood here during his lifetime and that he did make use of it.

The building we see today had come into existence by late Georgian or early Victorian times. By then it included a plunge pool where the residents of Greenway House and their guests could 'take the waters'. 'Taking the waters' became fashionable when George III began bathing at Weymouth in the late 18th century. To get the full benefit from this activity, the water needed to be salt. Salt water from the river was readily available on the high tide.

Above the bathing room is a well-appointed saloon, complete with a balcony and two fireplaces to ward off the cool evening air. Surely a place to leave the world behind and submit to the tranquillity of the waters beyond, whilst sipping one's chocolate, newly arrived from the Caribbean.

In more recent times, the Boathouse was simply a place of recreation. In the 20th century, it was to be known to millions of Agatha Christie readers as the place where Marlene Tucker was strangled in *Dead Man's Folly* – a strange fictional identity for such a real and timeless place.

The Battery

Formerly known as Goose Acre, this area has a romantic feel and is backed by a particularly large rocky outcrop. Dittisham can be glimpsed up river, whilst the closer Anchor Stone, in front, is a rock on which recalcitrant wives are said to have been tied. Today, only herons and seals stake their claim. This bastion dates from the early 18th century and may have been built as a Napoleonic defence in the 1790s. The path leading off towards Dittisham is in part hewn from bedrock and part edged with laurel. Tree roots and craggy outcrops can be slippery when wet.

Above View to Waddeton boathouse from Greenway Estate

Right Camellia hagoromo

The River Walk

Once leading from Greenway Quay to Maypool and beyond, the path now winds with the river. Terraces lined in parts by retaining walls between the river and the house hint at remnants of more formal features, possibly even the garden worked on by Spanish prisoners of war in the 16th century under Sir John Gilbert.

In 1588, Sir John was assigned responsibility for 160 Spanish prisoners of war captured by Sir Francis Drake with their Armada ship. The ship was moored in the Dart below Greenway, and Sir John used the prisoners to landscape the garden. However, it is difficult to know what this work achieved.

The Camellia Garden

A splendid sight in the spring, this garden has an enchantment all year round, and is a magnificent place to sit and watch the world drift by. Amongst the camellias is a splendid *Gevuina avellana,* 'the Chilean nut tree', and a 'Cork oak', *Quercus suber.*

The garden once housed a greenhouse with a 'hot wall' to protect tender plants, perhaps very early plantings of camellias, which in the mild Devon climate soon proved hardy enough to live outdoors.

Through the arch past the elegant curved wall, a gentle climb takes one past a sentinel row of lime trees. The path then steepens slightly, and arrives back at the Stable Block.